Att Soulmate

Manifest Love and a Relationship

Using the Power of the Universe

and the Law of Attraction

Sarah O. Annie

Table of Contents

Bluesource And Friends

This book is brought to you by Bluesource And Friends, a happy book publishing company.

Our motto is **"Happiness Within Pages"**
We promise to deliver amazing value to readers with our books.
We also appreciate honest book reviews from our readers.

Connect with us on our Facebook page www.facebook.com/bluesourceandfriends and stay tuned to our latest book promotions and free giveaways.

Don't forget to claim your FREE books!

Brain Teasers:

https://tinyurl.com/karenbrainteasers

Harry Potter Trivia:

https://tinyurl.com/wizardworldtrivia

Sherlock Puzzle Book (Volume 2)

https://tinyurl.com/Sherlockpuzzlebook2

Also check out our best seller book

https://tinyurl.com/lateralthinkingpuzzle

s

Introduction

Congratulations on getting *"Attracting Your Soulmate: Manifest Love and a Relationship Using the Power of the Universe and the Law of Attraction!"*

Being in love and finding love has become such a complicated thing in this day and age. Some people meet and instantly fall in love, and some take time before building a connection with one another. Other people spend a long time before they find the right match for them. This book will seek to explain how the law of attraction plays an essential role in the dating life of individuals.

In this book, you will get to understand what the law of attraction is and why it is a powerful tool in your dating life. The book explains how good vibes and the choice of words you use will determine which direction your dating life takes. Each chapter that you read here will give you a better understanding of how you can attract your soulmate and how the power is all in your hands. The information written in this book is not the only information available on the topic. However, the author of the book has researched from different sources and come up with content that is deemed to be truthful to give you insight on the topic.

The author hopes that his book will be useful and will help you toward your journey of dating and discovery. The author will not be responsible for any of the actions that an individual takes after reading this book.

Thank you for taking the time to read "*Attracting Your Soulmate: Manifest Love and a Relationship Using the Power of the Universe and the Law of Attraction!*" There are a lot of other books online that you could have chosen, but you preferred this one. You are appreciated!

Chapter I: What is the Law of Attraction and Why is It so Powerful?

The Law of Attraction—You have probably heard of it and maybe thought it sounded absurd and brushed it off. Well, the reality is that the Law of Attraction is an existing truth. The whole idea of the Law of Attraction is to harness the power of positive thinking to live a happier and more fulfilled life.

In a nutshell, the Law of Attraction is a belief that positive thoughts bring positive experiences in someone, while negative thoughts bring negative experiences alike. The whole concept is from the view that people and the ideas they have come in the form of pure energy. This energy will attract, hence, having positive energy in your life will result in your overall wellbeing in your relationships, health, and your wealth.

The Principles of the Law of Attraction

Principle 1: Like Attracts Like

Our bodies are filled with vibrations. Every feeling or emotion occurs to us in some form of energy, and it is channeled out of the body through vibrational frequencies. For instance, good health can only be achieved in an environment with high vibration frequencies, while diseases can only thrive in an environment with low vibration frequencies.

Similar vibrational frequencies of the various aspects of our lives attract each other. For instance, if you show love, you will draw more love. If you are afraid, more experiences that cause fear will occur to you. If you focus more on what you lack, that "lack" frequency will attract more of itself.

In general, anything you focus your attention and energy on will always grow.

Principle 2: The Vibrational Frequencies we experience originate from your emotions and thoughts

Thoughts and feelings always go hand in hand. What we think affects what we feel. Likewise, what you feel most of the time influences what goes through your mind. You can have better control of your emotions by having control over your thoughts. You can attract more positive energy by changing your thinking. Having positive thoughts is essential because it results in a burst of positive emotions.

The reverse works similarly. When you spend much of your time thinking of negative things, then you can only expect to draw negative emotions.

If you take a close look at those people you consider to be happiest around you, you will notice that they are always grateful—grateful for the things they have no matter how small they might seem to be. Such people have mastered the art of positive thinking. There is no way you can expect to experience happiness, satisfaction, and fulfillment if you are not grateful.

Your goal should be to always emit high vibrations from within you. While you cannot avoid negative emotions completely, your aim should be to build a strong positive vibrations antenna. Make the universe work for your good.

Principle 3: The language of your inner being is expressed through emotions

Understanding this concept can truly light up your world. Your inner being is the part of you that desires joy and love. It is the part that wants you to see yourself as a lovable and worthy person full of positive beliefs and emotions.

When your inner being is not aligned with what you are thinking or feeling, you experience this as a negative emotion. You somewhat feel separated from your inner self. The Law of Attraction calls for you to aim at reaching a place where the alignment you have with your inner body exists.

Principle 4: Change your focus, change your reality

Focusing on positive thinking and feelings will eventually result in thinking and feeling positive. It sounds absurd, but it's true.

For instance, if you have a problem that has been bothering you for a while, when you focus on the effects of the problem on your life and meditate on the negative impact of the problem, you will amplify your negative emotions. That will not cause the problem to go away. It might even get worse. But if you choose to approach the problem from a "How can I solve the problem?" perspective, then you will attract solutions that could help you resolve the issue. Solving the problem, in turn, changes your reality.

There is a quote by Ilan Shamir that goes like this: "A thousand things were right today." Reminding yourself this every day will help you have a more positive outlook of life.

Principle 5: Things won't manifest instantly

Mastering the art of emotional control and positive thinking is not something that happens overnight. It is a goal achieved by taking small, progressive steps. The small investments in learning how to shift your energy and thoughts will result in a positive outlook of life.

Let's face it, you cannot get rid of negative thoughts and emotions completely. What you can do is learn how to shift your focus from all that is going wrong in your life to all that is going right. Sometimes, it can be tough, especially if there is not much going right in your life. But by consciously working on changing your thoughts and emotions, it will get more comfortable for you. You will begin to be more grateful even for the smallest of things which will, in turn, result in a happier and more vibrant life for you.

You can commence your journey to emotional freedom and a world full of high-frequency positive vibrations by doing some simple practices. Some of the top three simple practices you can adopt are the following:

- **Write down things to be grateful for**

  Being grateful even for the smallest of things can help you harness positivity. Endeavor to be thankful, especially when you find it hard to be grateful.

- **Move your body**

  You can release your body of negative energy stored in it by moving your body. You can do exercises or dance. The important thing is to keep your body in motion.

- **Meditate**

Mediation helps you have a grip on your thoughts, hence giving you more control over what you think.

Chapter II: Choice of Words Matter Because They Manifest

Words are the beginning of everything. There is so much power that lies in words. Their influence is strong enough to manifest or take shape in the material world.

Words are a blend of sound and vibrations that have meaning. The nature of the vibration is what creates the meaning of what is within and around us. It is safe to say that words are life. They are the creators of our reality. They are our reality.

Now, think of this: if the words you speak every day are the creators of your reality, how powerful are they? Imagine the number of possibilities this creates. If words have the power to create the world around us, isn't it wise to pick and speak only the best of words to create the best reality?

Words first form in our minds, then we decide whether to express them with sound or store them in our memory as our thoughts. The previous chapter emphasized the importance of having a grip on our thoughts, as they are what influence our emotions. If you come to think of it, your thoughts appear in the form of words. As such, while the words you speak are essential, the words you think are more important.

Beware of the Power Your Words Hold in Determining Your Reality

When you continuously say disempowering things to yourself, you manifest them even without your knowledge. "I lack this," "I wish I had that," "I am not good at this," and many alike things might seem like simple phrases that acknowledge your reality. While that may have some truth, those words yield negativity, and without knowing, the lacking and the wishing become part of your existence. The reality is a manifestation of your past thoughts, inactions, and actions. As such, if you genuinely want to change your perception and live in a world you desire, change your beliefs by changing the words you associate with things.

Just thinking and saying positive words is not the end of it all. Your words should be accompanied by intentional action. Your positive thinking and words you speak will result in you emitting positive vibrations that will motivate you to take action. If you continuously choose words that dull the color of your reality, chances are you will not find sufficient motivation from within you to act intentionally toward changing your reality.

Choose Your Words Wisely

The world as it is today is full of chaos. There is so much going on, mostly negative things, that it is quite difficult to see the good things happen around you. The effect this has had over the years is that people have become conditioned to only talk about the problems and misfortunes around them. The impact this has—complaining and lamenting about our lives—is that, through words, they become a reality when told to others. Sometimes people say things one too many times, so that they become a reality even in the mind of those who are listening.

If you genuinely want to live the best life, is it, in any way, beneficial to keep reminding yourself and those around you how miserable your life is? Do you want to tell your family and friends that you are bored, that you failed, that you can't find love? These words create the life you are living now. When you speak them, they will only amplify the presence of that situation in your life.

From today, henceforth, choose your words consciously before you speak. Choose words that spark optimism and positivity when describing your life. While doing so, avoid those words that put you in a prison and limit your control over what is happening in your life. They will only strip you of the ability to manifest a reality you want to live.

It is always best to take a moment and think through what you are going to say before you say it. Pick those words that paint the perfect picture of the reality you would love, then speak.

Affirm Who You Are

The words "I am who I am and what I am" are compelling when it comes to affirming your hopes, dreams, and successes. The words "I am" hold incredible power. These two words, as short as they are, have the power to shape what your reality looks like. "I am ugly," "I am fat," "I am sad," "I am confident," "I am beautiful." How you end the "I am…" statement influences how you look at yourself and the truth you are choosing to believe. The words following these two magic words influence your reality.

Well, if you love yourself, which you should, you should choose to hold yourself with high regard. You should make it your priority to associate yourself with positivity. You should choose words that affirm your value and worth as a person—words that create a beautiful reality, and those that spark positive thoughts motivate you to act toward making your reality that which you want it to be.

Mean What You Speak

As stated a little earlier, always take a moment to think of the best words to use before you open your mouth to speak. Before speaking, ask yourself why you want to say what you want to say, and how it will influence your happiness and wellbeing.

Taking a moment to ask yourself these two questions will have you being intentional with what you say. Anything that is said births belief which, in turn, births motivation for you to speak and act positively. Be brave and loving with your choice of words. Always remember that your words are your world.

Your desires can be made manifest. The power lies in your words, and it starts in your mind. The words you think influence what you feel and believe. When you speak what you believe, you manifest the power of creation through those very words.

Chapter III: Understanding Yourself and What Kind of Lover You Are

Love begins from within before being shared out to the world. It should be your goal, and everyone's on the face of the earth, to live a life of love. For you to love better, you first have to know how to love yourself, and to love yourself better, you need to understand the kind of lover you are.

There are six (6) types of love. It sounds silly, but it is true. Each of these types of love is associated with different characteristics. Understanding the different traits and the critical attributes of the different kinds of love will help you know yourself better and the kind of lover you are. The knowledge will also help you love yourself and approach your romantic relationship with better insights.

Most people have a little bit of each of the types of love discussed below. But the one which you resonate the most is probably your dominant style of love.

Eros: The Physical Lover

The Eros type of love is one that attracts you to physically attractive people. The Eros type is always eager to get into intense and passionate relationships. Such persons thrive on an emotional high, and the feeling of love is usually most intense during the initial stages of the relationship.

While they can be intense lovers, physical lovers tend to be hooked on people's looks. They have some addiction to newness, which often leads them to lose interest in relationships quickly.

Mania: The Passionate Lover

Manic lovers are very demanding, outright possessive, and codependent. In relationships, they always have this intense need to be in control. They can be quite possessive and overly curious about their partner and what they are doing at every single moment. Most manic lovers find it hard to trust and can get hurt quite easily, since they often seek validation through their relationships.

Agape: The Unselfish Lover

These are unselfish lovers. These types of lovers focus more on giving rather than receiving. Their love is always unconditional. They always put the needs of their partner ahead of their own. Unselfish love is excellent and seems appealing. However, if only one of the parties in the relationship is the giver while the other just a receiver, issues with codependency will always arise.

Pragma: The Practical Lover

A pragma lover always looks for a person who fits a particular image. You know you are a pragma lover when you select a partner based on something they have; it can be age, physical attractiveness, financial abilities, spiritual background, or any other characteristics.

The main attributes of pragma lovers are that they are highly rational, they make use of empirical knowledge in their dating, and they are always keen to weigh their options before committing to getting into a relationship with someone.

Ludus: The Game Player

These are the types of lovers w view relationships as fun and casual engagements. As the name hints, those manifesting this type of love prefer playing games and entering into relations with the aim of just having fun. Commitment is their last objective.

It can be a bit hard to trust Ludus lovers. Those in relationships with Ludus lovers often have concerns about them cheating. The main attributes associated with Ludus lovers are that they are highly self-sufficient, they share little information about themselves, and they tend to portray narcissistic qualities.

Storge: The Compassionate Lover

With storgic lovers, they always strive to engage in relationships that are based on shared values, friendship, goals, and how compatible they are with their partner. They are a blend of agape and pragma types of lovers.

Physical attractiveness is not always a primary attribute storgic lovers are keen to find. In addition, most couples who have stayed together for a while, most of the time, end up being compassionate lovers. They are dependable and stable, they are not moved easily with temporary excitements and emotions, and high levels of trust often characterize their relationships.

Now that you have understood the different types of love and have probably figured the kind of lover you are, the next thing is to learn how to attract the right kind of love. Here are some tips to get you going with the same.

- **Be authentic**

  Authenticity is one of the most important things to focus on for genuine love to thrive. You will only understand who you are by being sincere and trustworthy. It is also the path that attracts true love.

  Besides, being authentic means not faking imperfections. It means being true to what really makes your heart beat. It means not shifting your passions and desire for the sake of pleasing others but, instead, doing that which pleases your heart. Be unapologetic about who you are inside.

- **Be your best self**

  If you love yourself, you will do everything to be the best version of yourself. It only makes sense to be the best version of yourself if you want to be the best for someone else.

Being the best version of you means taking care of your body, mind, and soul. It means investing in your personal growth, improving on your weaknesses, and striving to live a life of authentic joy, purpose, and grace.

- **Confidence**

  Confidence is your secret love magnet. You must live each day being confident in the decisions you make and the abilities you possess. Also, be confident in your authentic self, and be open to sharing with the world this part of you. When people see the confidence you have in yourself, they will naturally grow to love you for who you are.

- **Be open**

  You can only connect with others when you are open with them. Be ready to start conversations even with strangers. When you share, you open ports of connection, which attracts love.

- **Be happy**

  Everyone wants to be happy and be around happy people. The trick to this is simple: focus your energy on doing things that make you happy.

Understanding the kind of lover you are, coupled with being confident and open about your authentic self, is equal to self-love. Self-love is all about being you unapologetically.

Chapter IV: Letting Go of the Past and Getting a Clean Slate

The actions and inactions of your past determine your present. Of course, by living today, you would like your future to be a much better one than what your present is. That means you need to make conscious decisions today that will propel you toward living that better life in future.

One of the critical decisions to be made at present is to let go of the past and get a clean slate. Carrying around dysfunctional relationships, grudges, broken agreements, and all manner of harmful dirt from the past only serves to damage the strong foundation for a happier future life you are trying to achieve.

Letting go of the past doesn't have to be a hard task or experience. If anything, letting go of the baggage feels like having a heavy load lifted off you. You get to regain peace and comfort, and the freedom that the hurtful experience has robbed from you.

Before Letting Go

What happens when you want to let go of the past hurts and burdens is that all of them (the things have been weighing you down) will run through your mind, and they will seem huge as if they are part of you. They will tell you not to let them go. It can be a tough phase, and you will hate your mind for this.

What you should do is condition your mind to let go of these outdated beliefs. Remember the power of words? When you speak and tell your brain not to hold on the negative thoughts, with time, your mind will learn to let go.

How to Achieve a Clean Slate

The remainder of this chapter is going to focus on the practical ways you can use to achieve a clean slate. Let's jump right into it.

Identify the things that are holding you back

The first step toward cleaning your past is identifying those things that are holding you back. Most will occur to you quickly, but you may not realize that some things are holding you back. To do this, take time and think through all the things you would like to let go. Write them down if possible. Once you have listed them down, specify what you would like to change in your life, and list down the actions you can take to help you achieve that goal.

You really can't overcome what you do not know. That is the whole essence of this first step.

End what you need to end

As dramatic as it sounds, you need to conclude that which needs to end. Most people tend to fuel and breathe more life into things that they should have let go a long time ago. The exciting thing is that you always know these things, and you always know you need to stop holding onto them. Once the time has come for something to come to an end, be faithful enough to yourself and put an end to it.

Forgiveness

There are different levels of forgiveness. The first and most important one is self-forgiveness. For you to let go of the past, you need to forgive yourself for the mistakes you made. Forgiving yourself is very important, as it is by forgiving yourself that you can forgive others.

Forgiving others means accepting that they are fellow humans who have their weaknesses just like you. Forgiving those who wronged you in the past gives you the freedom to feel happy, and it shouldn't just be a single act. Forgiveness should be a constant ongoing commitment through to your last day on Earth. It means that when you choose to forgive someone, you will dig up their faults in the future and hold their mistakes against them.

Meditate

Meditation is a way for you to become alive and in the moment. It gives you the opportunity to step out of the past and into the present. Through meditating, you allow your universe to achieve calmness. You get to understand that you are exactly where you need to be and that you cannot change the past. It gives you a clean slate and allows you to write a new story in a way you desire.

Face your fears

When you face your fears, they become less scary. The trick is pretty simple: try doing something you have always been scared to do once, and then do it again. Now, do it every day. You can decide to do as many things that scare you as possible.

The thing about facing your fears is, you will realize the things you fear may not be as scary as they seem. And even if they are, you can always get past them. Facing your fears gives you the courage to confront the challenges that have been holding you back from the past.

Love yourself more

This might sound a bit weird, but love conquers all. You literally can love yourself into freedom. Loving yourself means doing that which is best for your overall wellbeing. If you have to tramp your ego and call that person, with whom you have a rough relationship, do it. Loving yourself equips you to deal with pain and suffering. It leads you to an understanding that the steps you take are for your overall wellbeing and peace of mind.

Another significant benefit of learning to love yourself more is, it helps you understand that while pain is inevitable, suffering is optional. When you don't love yourself enough, you will allow yourself to dwell in the painful experiences of the past leading to your present distress. But through love, you get to understand that harboring the pain of memories only draws life out of you. Through that love, you will get to stop fueling the anger and resentment that causes more pain.

A clean slate is very important if you want to live your best. While letting go of the past can be a complicated process, achieving a clean slate is even more fulfilling.

Chapter V: Visualization - Visualize What Your Perfect Lover Will be Like

One of the top priorities of many people is finding their significant other. People spend so much time and energy to find that perfect match for them. Most end up meeting someone and like each other for a while, but then it never lasts for long.

Well, maybe the problem is the lack of a clear image of how they would want their perfect lover to appear. That is where the concept of visualization comes in. If you are one of those people looking for a lover, then you definitely should try visualization.

Visualization entails you to form an image in your mind of what your ideal lover would look like. It is like planting a mental seed. When you visualize your perfect lover and act, you actually can manifest what you have imagined. By visualizing the kind of person you want, you can attract people with the attributes you have visualized, in real life.

Simple Steps You Can Follow to Visualize and Manifest your Ideal Mate

The first step towards creating a perfect visual picture of how you would like your ideal lover to be is to ask yourself what you want. It is essential to take your time and be honest with yourself about what you want. Describe them in detail. Be as specific as possible, and specify as many attributes as possible that you would like them to have.

Other than asking yourself what you would like him or her to be, take time and consider how you would wish other people, especially those close to you, to describe them. When you get a soulmate, they become part of your world—a world that comprises of you and those around you too. That is why it is also important to describe how you would want other people to view them and your relationship.

After outlining the things you want in your lover, now do the reverse. Outline those attributes you would like them not to possess. It is important to understand yourself when answering this question. Know the things you are willing to compromise and those that you cannot compromise in the relationships you engage in.

An example of a list is this: "I would want a lover who is attractive, honest, kind, generous, understanding, fun, and outgoing. I do not want a lover who is unfaithful, hurtful, insecure, dishonest, and jealous." Feel free to elaborate on as much as possible when outlining these attributes.

With your list at hand, you are now ready for visualization. However, while you need to have a list of what you would not like your lover to have, your focus will mainly be on the positive things—the attributes you would like them to have. The reason for this is simple: investing your time and energy on what you do not want attracts those negative attributes to you.

Visualization Process

Scenario 1: A man meeting his ideal woman

The first step in the visualization process is to relax. Get to a calm and peaceful place with no distractions. Close your eyes and clear your mind of any other distractive thoughts. Breathe. This first step is pretty standard for any visualization process.

Now, pick an ideal place you would like to meet your perfect lady. For instance, you picture yourself in a restaurant setting. Build that image in your mind, being careful to be as detailed as possible. For example, picture the setting by looking at how the lights appear and how the tables are arranged. You can also look at the color of the walls. Picture the number of people in the restaurant. What are you eating? Who is with you? What kind of clothes are you wearing? Which waiter served you? Now, picture your ideal woman getting into the restaurant. Imagine where she sits. Is she near you or at the corner table? What is she wearing? How do her earrings look and what does she order?

The next step is to play that scenario as if you are watching a movie where you and your perfect lover are the main characters. Get into the moment and act it out in your mind. Approach her, say hi, and engage in a conversation. Notice how she behaves; the way she responds warmly at your talk is striking. You make silly jokes that she genuinely finds funny. Picture how she's laughing so loudly. Play the scene as you would want it to happen.

Now, bring yourself to her presence, and not just someone watching from afar. There is a transition from a third-person point of view to a first-person point of view. Keep the conversation flowing and feel the warmth from her side. Feel that you are connecting and that she is making you feel relaxed and alive. Do these for a few minutes then let it go from your mind. Let that perfect image of a perfect encounter with your ideal lover slip slowly from your mind.

Scenario 2: A woman meeting her perfect man

The first thing is to get into a calm spot and clear your mind of any distractions. Take deep breaths and begin visualizing your ideal man.

Let's say you would like to meet your ideal man when you are relaxing at the beach over the weekend. You are there in your bikini and sunglasses basking in the sand. There are several other people on the beach, but not so many. To your right, some kids are building a sand castle, and to your left, a couple is walking holding hands. Then you see this handsome man coming out of the water with his surfboard. You hear the noise of the kids and people chatting, and the waves hitting the shore. You smell the air, and then your eyes meet.

He comes straight to you and borrows your sunscreen lotion. In the process, you begin a conversation, and it turns out to be fun. You like him. You can't seem to stop smiling. You are comfortable around him. Take yourself from a third-person point of view to a first-person and feel the moment. After a few minutes, allow the image to slip away slowly.

As you go about visualizing your perfect lover, remember that mental images alone are not enough. Visualization has to be accompanied by the right action.

Chapter VI: Understanding Energy and Vibrations to Resonate with the Universe

You exist in the universe not just as a physical being in a physical space but, also, as energy and vibration in a vibrational and energetic universe. The way you connect and communicate with the world is by being an energy transmitter. Nikola Tesla says, "If you want to know the secrets of the universe, think in terms of energy, frequency, and vibration."

While the entire existence of humans in the universe is in the form of energy and vibrations, learning and mastering the art of living as vibrational beings has always proven to be elusive to many. This chapter focuses on giving you a better understanding of how to connect with the universe and your partner by signaling the right types of vibrations, and absorbing and releasing energy into the universe in the right way.

Like Signals Attract

Have you ever entered into a room, a place, or joined a group of people and your reaction and the feelings inside you suddenly changed? That is the power of vibrations you and the people in that space are emitting. When you hang around people who are full of energy and positivity, you are probably going to feel the same way. If you are used to complaining and hating, then you probably are going to attract people who hate and complain, since that is the signal you are sending into the universe.

As such, it is essential to match your energy to those things you would like to manifest in your life. A happier and more fulfilled life is characterized by the presence of vibrations of high frequency and energy. If you want to prove the truth in this, look at the people who are depressed or sick. They always have deficient energy, and it can be challenging to vibe with them. But those people who are healthy and happy are always filled with a lot of energy. They are vibrant all of the time.

So now, how do you raise your vibrations to resonate more with the universe? Well, here are some tips for you.

Write it down

If you want the universe to act in your favor, write down what you want from it. When you pen down the goals and desires of your life, you start producing signals that bring you close to those things that you desire. Writing your desires down is somewhat like tuning a guitar. It sets the stage for you to achieve the tune you want.

Visualization

The more time you spend visualizing what you would want to happen in your life, the more you begin to feel like that mental picture is part of your reality. Visualization helps you to align your energy and desires with the vibrations of the things you want from the universe.

Affirm yourself

There is power in words of affirmation. Affirmations help to remove the stumbling blocks that block your manifestations. Assertions are a way of matching your energy and vibration frequencies with those things you would like to manifest in your life.

Feel and feel some more

Feelings are crucial in tuning your vibrations. While you can think and visualize a whole lot, unless you see your desires manifesting, your vibrations won't go high enough to match the vibrations of the things you desire.

Gratitude

The secret to perfect harmony with the universe is gratitude. Appreciation calls for you to be thankful for the things you have now and the space you are in at the moment. Gratefulness, in turn, yields higher vibrational frequencies, making you feel happier, energetic, and more fulfilled.

Love hard

The thing about love is that it causes everything to move. It brings harmony and gentle flow to things.

Hate, on the other hand, takes so much energy and only serves to block vibrations. As such, raising your vibrations calls for you to radiate love every day. And the universe will always send love right back to you. Amazing, right? Above all, strive to be the most authentic version of yourself.

"When we allow ourselves to be authentically free, it raises our vibration" – Alaric Hutchinson, Living Peace.

Vibrations that Resonate with Your Partner

The person you would like to attract is a person whom you would love to share with your life's experiences. They have to be a person who matches your vibrations and energy. They have to be someone whom you vibe with effortlessly.

Using the knowledge that "like attracts like," you should strive to emit signals that attract a potential partner with whom you will vibe. In the previous chapter, you listed attributes you would love your perfect lover to have. But people will not have those attributes written on their foreheads. So, the only way to attract them is by producing vibration signals that communicate those values. If you want a fun person, start doing fun activities. If you desire to get a humble person, begin by being humble yourself. If you want someone who is faithful, show faithfulness in the relationships and engagements you are in at the moment.

Shifting Your Vibrations

Your vibrations can be shifted pretty quickly. It only takes a song, a smile, or some form of a motion to change your vibrations. However, these create a temporary change in your vibrations which, in turn, results in only temporary change that doesn't last long. But if you want to shift your equilibrium, you need to do more.

Shifting your equilibrium means completely blocking the signals from the situations you would want to change. It can be done in two ways. First, is entirely shifting your vibrations and regularly transmit new signals. Eventually, you will begin to repel those vibrations that are not in harmony with your "new" vibrations. In so doing, you will achieve a new equilibrium.

The other way is by changing your environment completely. You probably are where you are, because you and the environment you are in are producing similar signals. If you want a new norm, try changing

your environment entirely to that which you desire—
of course, a better one.

Accomplishing these things may not be as simple as it
sounds. It takes time and intentional dedication to
understand the universe and speak its language. You'll
struggle and stumble many times, but when you do
understand how to communicate with the universe,
the rewards are astounding.

Chapter VII: Manifesting Love

Sometimes, it can be quite overwhelming when everyone else seems like they have figured everything out with regards to their love life. Well, now you know the power of manifesting. If you find yourself in such a situation, don't stare into the void of loneliness. Fill that void yourself. You fill that void by accepting that you are complete and that you lack nothing. This acceptance will send out the right signal, and the right kind of people will be attracted to you.

Practices to Help You Manifest Love

Be grateful for your active relationships that are thriving

If you want to manifest love, do it first by vibrating gratitude. It might sound pretty simple, but given we live in a world full of negativity with everyone complaining about all that is wrong, it can be tough to find reasons to be grateful for your relationships.

Some relationships you can consider are your most valued friendships, your relationships with your family, and your relationship with yourself. Be grateful for these relationships.

However, it doesn't have to be limited to your relationships with human beings. You can go out and appreciate nature. The point is to find a reason to be grateful. When you signal gratefulness, you attract love.

Let go of your judgmental self

One of the ways people lose out on experiencing true love and genuine connections is by being overly judgmental of others. You might be so fixated on what you want them to be that you fail to see who they are. Being judgmental is just amplifying pessimism in you, which is a form of negative energy.

When you avoid being judgmental, you open up an avenue for love to thrive. You get to accept that things will never be perfect, and that gives you a chance to be happy. And with a happy soul, you send a signal to the world that you want some more.

Avoid selling yourself short

You shouldn't just settle for anything that comes your way. You need to have standards. You need to hold yourself in high regard and avoid any form of mediocrity from yourself and other people. If you have relationships that are not good for you, walk away without apologies.

Selling yourself short is a way of accepting less and being comfortable with things that suck the life out of you. The interesting thing about humans is that deep down within, we always know when we deserve better. As such, your aim should be to believe in your worth and go for relationships that add value to you.

Set yourself in the right path

The purpose of getting in a relationship that is founded on love is not to fill a gap in your life. Instead, it is to get this extra ingredient in your life called love that will help you live fully. It is to enhance your experience. That should be your goal.

If you focus on trying to find love because you feel like you need to fill a gap in your life, chances are you will attract the wrong person to yourself. As such, set yourself on the right path by having the right goal and objective.

It is always good to write down your objective. What do you want from someone? When you approach this from the point of honesty while understanding what you want, the universe will listen. The idea is to get to a point where you are more than ready for when your soulmate comes along.

Again, visualization

The essence of visualization could not be stressed any further. In your mind, what does love look like? How do you want your soulmate to love you? How does their love feel to you? Does it spark joy, excitement, relief, happiness, and contentment?

Visualization is all about living the dream in your head. Picture yourself at that moment when you have already found your lover. Picture yourselves together over and over again. Eventually, the signals you send to the universe through that process will attract that kind of love you so desire to you.

Tell the world what you want

Well, continued affirmation and visualization are great, but they alone are not enough to manifest love. They have to be accompanied by intentional action.

Once you feel that you are ready to meet your soulmate, do not shy off from telling the world what your intentions are. It does not mean you have to announce to everyone you know that you are looking for someone. Only inform the ones closest to you, whom you trust. Dare to tell them of the attributes you are looking for in your lover.

The point is, people will not read your mind and know your intentions if you do not tell them what you want. If you are shy, then you probably might have a more difficult time finding the love you so desire.

However, you need to be assured in how you communicate your desires and interests. You need to sound confident and not needy. Otherwise, your quest might backfire.

Build a good life for yourself

One of the best strategies to follow when manifesting love in your life is merely building a good foundation for that love first. Build a purpose to live a life that you love, which is full of happiness and contentment. It is only when you have built a good life for yourself that you can invite others to share in your experience.

Manifesting love is not just about what you want. It is majorly about what you have. You find love by cultivating love, and that is possible by being in a position of authenticity and honesty. You find love by making sure that you have a strong foundation for that love to thrive when it finally comes around.

Chapter VIII: Taking Action Regardless of the Results

Filling your mind with all the positive words and even visualizing your soul mate is awesome. But they all amount to nothing if a solid action plan does not accompany them. Taking action is a way of manifesting that which you desire.

Nothing in this life is a guarantee. You can spend so much energy and effort getting something or achieving a particular goal but still end up failing. This fear of failure and getting hurt is what often hinders people from taking action.

Having come a long way, it only makes sense to try and try again, even when the results of your previous action were disappointing. You want to know why? Here is why.

- **No one is coming to live your life for you**

  As harsh as it may sound, you had better realize that no one will come out of the blue to pursue your dreams and desires for you. You need to make it part of your responsibility to accompany your desires with actions. After visualizing, tell your friends what you want in a partner and get their help in finding one if possible. Go on those dates. Conquer your fears.

- **What you know is pretty worthless if you do not apply it through your actions**

  You have taken your time to understand read and understand about The Law of Attraction. You have read further and realized that your words have a lot of power, and through words, you can manifest what you desire. You have read all manner of material, and you feel very motivated. But is that enough?

Reading and getting all the vital information is very necessary. It sharpens your thinking. But gathering all that knowledge does not replace action. There is no way of bypassing this fact. The reality is that if you do not actualize your expertise through your efforts, the knowledge remains to be intangible and powerless. It becomes useless.

- **We learn and understand by doing things**
  When you do things, that is when you get to master them even better. And the thing is, you can acquire knowledge from the same source as someone else. The content is pretty much the same. But that cannot be said about experiences since everyone is different. For instance, the experience you will get when you go on a date with one person is not the same

as the experience someone else will get when they go on a date with the same person.

When you do things, you discover that the reality is a bit different from all the theory you have been mastering from the books, blogs, seminars, and counseling sessions. Your results may not always be as you desire; you will realize that putting your knowledge into action is fun.

- **Boost your self-esteem**

  Earlier you learned that the good things in life are associated with high vibrations.

  Developing a habit of taking action will help in propelling you toward achieving the results you desire, while at the same time helping you boost your confidence and self-esteem. It, in turn, results in you producing vibrations of a higher frequency.

- **The clock never stops ticking**

Another important reason why you need to take action regardless of the result is the simple reality that time won't stop to wait for you. Neither can it be turned back. When you fail to act, you rob yourself of time.

Consider a person who wants to find a lover with whom they will share their life. If they sit in comfort of their home waiting for their soulmate to come, chances are they will end up missing out on ever meeting them. Even if they do meet later, they will have lost a significant amount of time that they would have enjoyed in the company of one another.

On the contrary, a person who decides to go out and look for their soulmate is likely to meet their soulmate much faster and get to experience their love for a more extended period.

The bottom line is that your life has an end. Your time is crucial and every moment you waste will not be recovered. As such, always purpose to take action toward the reality that you want to live.

- **Action gives satisfaction**
  There is a feeling of satisfaction that dawns on you when you know you have taken all the measures necessary toward achieving something. Acting gives you closure. You will live with the comfort of knowing whether your actions were good enough or not good enough to warrant you the results you got.

When you act, you get to know the outcome. You will not spend the rest of your life wondering what would have happened if you acted.

- **You develop a habit by taking action**

  Doing something just once or just a few times will not result in the manifestation of what you desire in life. For things to manifest, you must consistently take action and develop a habit out of it.

  For instance, if you want to be fit, meditating on what you need to do, and doing so for just one day will not yield the results you desire. To be fit, you need to do more than just meditating. You need to commit to going to the gym or to working out every single day until it becomes part of you or a habit.

- **Actions yield success**

Well, you might fail so many times, but unlike someone who doesn't take any action, you will eventually succeed. Every accomplishment is backed by action. Your efforts have to be intentional and in line with your goal. That is the only way you are going to manifest success, happiness, and love in your life.

The whole concept of taking action might seem scary to many. It is only the first step that is always scary. The more you act, the more confidence you get. You will try and fail so many times. An essential thing to do is to get up and try again; with great caution, having learned from the previous experience.

Chapter IX: Dating Tips (for Both Men and Women)

Dating is one of the most challenging phases when you are trying to start a new relationship. This is the time you are meeting this stranger to try and figure out if they are the perfect match for you. Of course, most of us are clueless about how to handle this phase.

This last section is going to equip you with tips and tricks to help you when you are in your dating phase. The tips are split for men and women. Let's dive into them.

Dating Tips for Men

Make the best first impression

First impressions matter a great deal. The first thing your date will see when she sets your eyes on you is how you have groomed yourself. She will notice how you have dressed and how clean you are. When going on a date, especially the first date, make an extra effort on how you dress up. While you love those rugged jeans, you might want to consider putting on better looking pants. Take a shower and clean your hair with a shampoo. Look your best.

Other than looking good, time keeping also matters a lot when going on dates. If you show up late for your date, you will give the impression that you are unreliable. You communicate that the date is not a top priority for you.

Therefore, dress well and show up on time.

Plan the date in a comfortable location

When choosing a place to hang out with your potential mate for your date, it is crucial to pick a place that gives you calmness and comfort.

Remember you are meeting a whole new being and the experience can make you nervous. You wouldn't want to appear nervous in front of your date now, would you?

Confidence matters a great deal

Confidence is outright attractive. You should wear it when meeting your date. If you are a shy person, take some time before the date and practice beforehand with people you do not know.

When on the date, be careful with the topics you choose to discuss. Avoid those dull topics. Pick subjects that keep the conversation going to avoid moments of awkward silence, when you talk about something that matters to you passionately.

Note: Your look and the location choice also have some influence on your level of confidence. When you look good, you feel good and are more confident.

The same applies to when you are comfortable with a particular space.

Give her a chance to talk

However much you love what it is you do, don't go on and on about it without giving her an opportunity to speak. Pause occasionally and ask your date about her. Listen to what she what she likes and loves. Show her you are interested in knowing about her just as she is about to know you. If you vibe, the chances are that she will say yes to a second date.

It is essential to listen to her when she talks. It is only through listening that you will get to know her well.

Do not use your phone

Turn off your phone when on your date. Give her your full attention. Picking up your phone several times while on a date is annoying. The distraction they bring lowers the quality of your time together.

Get help from your female friends

Well, if you are trying to understand women and how their mind works, why not seek help from them. If you are getting into the dating scene, get in touch with a close female friend and ask them for help. It could go a long way in helping you handle your dates more effectively.

Dating Tips for Women

Don't be afraid to make the first move

Men love it when women approach them first. It communicates the message that you are interested in them. So, if you notice a guy you like and he hasn't noticed you or hasn't made a move on you, don't be afraid to make the first move. He probably will be very impressed.

Be honest

While men are mostly attracted to physically attractive females, honesty is a virtue that ranks among the top three (3) things men look for in women. Therefore, don't go on a date with a guy with a fake version of yourself. Be authentic and honest.

Talk about your passions and interests

Men love women who know what they are doing— women who have a life of their own. On the first date, tell him about the things that interest you. Speak about your passions. These subjects give him an excellent initial picture of who you are. Also, it is effortless to have lively conversations around these topics.

Don't talk about your past relationships

Almost everyone has been into previous relationships that didn't work. The experiences were probably very hurtful to you. Now, if you are dating, it is important to remember that these events "happened" and are not "happening." What is happening is your date. Therefore, avoid talking about your failed relationships from the past. Such topics are a huge turn off for men.

Do not be who you think your date wants you to be

The whole point of going on a date is to establish if someone is the ideal person with whom you will share life. It means that you need to be an authentic version of yourself right from the beginning. Do not try to change your character to fit the image of the person you think your mind wants. If you do so, one day, you will drop the act and reveal your true self. That is the day everything you are trying to build will come crumbling down.

Well, the thing about dating and relationships is that there is no definite answer to how you will manage them. You get in and go with the flow. However, the point highlighted above can be beneficial if you are determined to create something beautiful.

Remember, your first encounter may not be what you desired. When your first date fails, keep your focus on what you want and be ready to go and try all over again.

Conclusion

If you are here reading this, then it means that you have reached the end of the book. Thank you for getting to the end of the book and congratulations on your journey toward attracting your soulmate. Everything needs a formula, and that includes love and dating. A lot of people get into the dating field without any guide at all, and they end up lucky in finding the right person for them. However, dating experience is not the same for everyone. Different individuals need a different kind of direction or an incentive to thrive in their journey toward finding the right person.

Reading "*Attracting Your Soulmate: Manifest Love and a Relationship Using the Power of the Universe and the Law of Attraction*" is the first step to attracting your soulmate. After reading this book, you can decide if you would like to seek further guidance. The author hopes that you were able to grasp some or all of the information that you need in your journey. Taking action should be the next step. Everything that you have read will be of great use if you implement it into your life.

Write down a plan on how you can go about changing things in your life to attract this special someone. I hope that your journey will be fruitful and that it will have a positive outcome. Get advice from a professional if you feel the need to do so and have a great experience.

I hope that this book has added some value to you. If it has, a great review on Amazon will be highly appreciated!

Sarah O. Annie

42394795R00052

Made in the USA
Middletown, DE
13 April 2019